THIS BOOK IS DEDICATED TO ETHAN AND ALEX.

COVER ART BY ROB KNAPP.

TOURNIQUET

Table of Contents

ALEX:

Lick your wounds, but don't live in them.

The Problem Is You

They are out there dying,
and I can't even get angry enough to pick up my sword.
Giving up this addiction because
these veins could not take anymore.
A hero's impulse is to do the right thing
no matter how the cards are dealt.
I'm not stupid enough to offend the gods,
but I'm smart enough to protect myself.
It's better to be friends than enemies.
And you probably shouldn't mix the two.
If everyone around you is a problem, then
I guess you know the problem is you.
I live the life of a smog monster.
Your skills are no match for me.
I cannot swallow.
My throat is swollen with fury.
All of this order offends me.
I'll smash it in a violent spree.
I feel my nature splinter.
The urge to slash is desolating.
My mouth is full of gravel.
I was dead the moment you arrived.
But whatever the threat you pose to me,
I trust you with my heart and my life.
Sympathy for the devil
is masochistic to say the least.
It puts me at a disadvantage
to wonder how scarred you might be.
The longer I am with you,
the less familiar you are.
The electricity snaps
and all my nerves misfire.

Victim of Circumstances

He's less of a fag than I am.
Yet I felt something was wrong.
I feel licks of white-hot pain.
You can't be awful if you aren't there.
But I'm not ready to get to know you.
A ghost in daylight.
Spiders eat their young.
It's your actions that make you good or evil.
You apologize to me because
justice is restoring order.
Do what's right, and the pieces
fall where they fall.
Slow progress is lasting progress.
There is no such thing as a final score.
All addicts have syphilis.
Paralyzing pain like a knee in your balls.
Just a victim of circumstances.
They make you feel less than human.
They make it a crime to be an addict.
Your cells are hungry in
your insect-like activity.
You want to break through to the surface.
You pretend it doesn't bother you, but
your heart wants to explode.
Isn't this hell?
The orgasm of a dying man.
Thick blood clots the needle.
Ants under your skin.
He might die only because he could
no longer stand to be in his body.
He's dripping blood
all over my freshly cleaned floor.

Con or Man

A predator is a predator
So I try not to move
These fuckers can smell fear
There is a difference in being
Perverted and abnormal
Sometimes it's subtle
I listen to you because
I am that afraid
I could only see his hands and mouth
You put everyone else first
You end up last
All pleasure is relief
When you stop growing you start dying
You spout ribbons of nonsense
Muttering into the silence
It swallowed you whole
The heavy breathing suddenly stopped
Your anxiety fed my own
You think you can control it but
Sometimes you don't want to control it
I took every punch so that
You wouldn't have to
You can either be a con or a man

Alex Lies

His hair in her face
Her foot in his shin
She screamed out her rage
And cursed him again

In a drug-filled haze
He didn't know when
He fell out of place and was
Consumed from within

She fell to her knees
An angel who sinned
She watches him bleed and knows
she can't save him

Visually Stimulated

How could I let you
Take on my suffering
Let you in to
Bear the weight of my agony
As usual, it's been too long
Though I always want the touch
I'll settle for a whore
Anything to feel loved
So visually stimulated
Deep as insanity
I took up too much space
Yet you always carried me
Why do I wait so long
Why do I play along
I want you to be the one
I put my mouth upon
My body cries out for relief
And my skin is ancient and cracked
I press the damage on
There's no turning back
Has my potential grown
Or am I still naïve and fake
You get your pleasure on
I make the same mistake
Why must it be so hard
Why do I long to be numb
Why do I fall for your charm
And let you rip me up
Pulling on sensitive parts
Eventually throwing up
A well-known tug at my heart
The whiskey makes me in love

Live

My father was a sociopath
My father's world was black
I used to curse my old man
But I take those curses back

I used to curse him every day
And hope he was in hell
But now I find my anger gone
I wish I wished him well

My father died in the living room
My father died alone
And as my loved ones surround me
I see I have grown strong

I can hate, and curse, and scream
And wish that he would die
But I would carry that poison he had
And it would destroy me from the inside

I do not know how my father felt
I'll never understand
But the greatest revenge I can now have
Is to live the best I can

Poison Underneath the Skin

I'm so tired I can taste my bones.
It feels like poison underneath the skin.
Sweat it out, if you can.
Some days it seems like my own body
wants to destroy me.
What's left of my heart is
made of light.
My body is without veins.
Electricity flows through me.
It's that insomnia painted silence…
that bites through my dreaming.
My skin is mutilated by hundreds of needles.
My love has grown restless.
Apollo's lament.
My dreams are just traces of some
other fool's delight.
It came in a swarm of blood.
And I understood it down to my core.
My tears muddy your clothes.
And I play with the troll under the bridge.
He knows the world is not noble.

Telling My Lie

Through the barbed wire you
hesitate.
I suffocate, but not as fast as you would have.
Not as fast as your chaos spreads.
When I need you, you're not here.
Reach into this nightmare and find me.
I know you are lying because
you're telling my lie.
Resentment will kill you as fast
as your vanity.
Take the cotton out of your ears and
put it in your mouth.
You've got nothing to feed on.

Through the Decay

It seems there are two of you
through the decay.
It has always been your way or none.
God please forgive them if they disobey.
So, maybe their courage has worn pretty thin.
But when they step out of line you make
examples of them.
You will beat them & bleed them
until they can barely move.
But still in your mind you
have something to prove.
You've got no time for living or breathing.
Pull the rope around his neck.
Why can't they shut up and
show some respect?
You've got your hand on his chest.
You want to give him a job.
Inside I think you want him
dead on the floor.
Standing right beside you,
I have something to say.
It's something I could never mention before.
So, I'm in too deep...
but how deep is too deep?
I will always crave more.
This place is a different place today.
My life—a strange life.
It doesn't even feel the same.
I will never get it right.
I am a new person today.
The haze has cleared away.
Guessing gets me nowhere when
I don't know the game.
Last night our conversation
made perfect sense.
But now I have changed and
I can't be near you anymore.
You were just a bump
in my sobriety.

Drunk AA

It's like walking to an AA meeting
drunk—you can't understand it.
It seems like just your luck. You
pawned all precious stones for a
moment of peace. It filled you
up as you prayed for some release.
I thought I was honest because
I didn't tell a lie. I just drank
enough to get me by. I remember
well that first night in jail. The son
of a bitch would not shut
up. His face made of stone because
he doesn't feel well. The mirage
is clutching this poisoned cup.
Bloody bones, shred me with your
Claws. The grinding of knives—
the screaming fall. The edge is blunt.
With a wolfish grin the meddling
devil invites you in. There's a
crack in my wall and the sea
rushes in. The flesh itches and burns.
The armor's grown thin.

Little Sister

When I say my little sister had cancer, most people don't understand. They think it is only bad in the end. They don't know that each day is hell, and every day is a reprieve. She never wanted anyone to see her sick and shaking. She never wanted anyone to know she lost control of her bladder, and couldn't empty her own bedpan. She was always cold and seemed to wear blankets for years. I had to watch her disappear—cheek sinking into jaw, and hands turning into small claws. She taught me people never stay… and you are never safe. Her own body was a violent prison.

Wake Up

I wake up quick
I couldn't find you
I wake up in jail
What did I do?
The blood on my hands
The dirt on my shoes
On my right thigh
A mysterious bruise
How long have I
Reeked of defeat?
He was kind and good
So why did I leave?
I stood in the rain
And never felt clean
Because I finally see
The problem is me

Clichés

The devil plays piano
in the bar on the corner.
There's nowhere I can put my foot
that isn't stepping on his tail.
The nail are always rusty here, but
I am trying to accept it.
You blame me for every horrid thing
I did to you in your mind--
the crimes I committed in your dreams.
Cut off from your mercy;
cut off from your grace.
You made a mess of my life, so
I made a mess of your face.
He speaks in clichés,
which pisses me off.
Cuz this ain't the movies, and
that ain't how people talk.
These people take everything so seriously.
You can't see the metaphor, and that's scary.
Odin leads the AA meeting, and
he tips his hat to me.
The penalty is too severe.
Deep sadness always follows the anger.
I'm all out of forgiveness, and the past
doesn't just slip through your fingers.
I'm missing the funeral, and
the guns all taste of copper.
Being a junky was never the problem.

Mental Twist

I cut off your head and
mount it on my wall.
Eyes too wide, as though
even in death you were surprised.
I light a cigarette and
stare at you.
Because I won, you bastard,
I won.
Then why is a scream trapped
in my throat?
I have proven even gods bleed.
I have you on your back.
My brain trembles and I
can't tell the mud from the blood.
You crawled out of the sea with
a message for me,
but I'd rather be chasing my shadow.
Your tongue is like an eel, and
just as cold.
Behind your eyes are more horrors
than I can imagine.
My hands are fists that
rage pours out of.
You blend in with the walls, but I
have the kind of face people notice.
I am studying the dawn.
Your dead face is pale and
shattered by drugs.
It was a mental twist that
maybe this time will be different.

IRONY

I hate irony
You told me to stay inside
but I didn't
Little did you know I've been
waiting for you all my life
I was following my path
You are good when you're sober
and even better when you're drunk
Your darkness
Your secret sickness
taught me how little I matter
I never could swim well, but I
sure knew how to float
How well do you know this room?
Well enough to leave?
Well enough to bleed?
You were never satisfied
by the dark
I can't destroy you but
I also can't blame you
I know there will always be
darkness, and I know the
creatures that live there
I can't feel a thing
You told me you'd killed before
I tasted rust and
the second time
I think I tried to run
You cornered me—yelling,
striking—but—
there was no pain
I had lost my focus and
become an animal
My fear never saved me

Spare A Penny

Not again.
Something hidden
right behind the eyes.
Spare a penny.
What are you hiding?
Your jealousy is
well documented.
I love you so much.
Turn off the sun and
stare through your cage.
I don't know how
to seduce you.
And here we try living
without the air.
How good are you at guessing?
Being tired makes you careless, but
bandages have many uses.
My laughter is my self-defense.
Bad chemicals and bad ideas
brew to poison the mind.
I laugh until pain
boils up inside me.
If you could choose who lives
and who dies that would
make you a monster.
A wound that's crusted over but
never really heals.

Shiver

Unlike some who would be crazy not to drink, I become crazy when I do. Touch
any part and the whole web shivers. I believe in inner distance, so I do not get fully
involved. A dark energy fills me like blood on the snow. But this is not my
tragedy. You have to look outside yourself.

Greta

She is a mask wearing a face.
They said you liked to make a mess.
A secret order.
You need the treatment of the sea.
I'm not worried about it—
It's a secret weapon.
It's not you this time;
don't be a priest.
I thought I was doing great
until I had that drink to celebrate.
It seems sadly ironic
what time will do to you--
Underwater portraits.
Enjoy the morning,
but you must die first.
It's an obligation.
Is there a language barrier?
It's more intimate than that.
Explore going off.
She was in my bedroom.
When I came into the room,
you weren't breathing.
How can you not remember?
Are you sick?
Did you get that leak fixed?
Maybe it's the tequila.
Or maybe it's just me.

Scabs

Every time she cuts herself
the wounds don't want to bleed.
She needs to show she's hurting;
to prove it physically.
Every time she cuts herself
my heart starts to crack.
If she slices in too deep
there is no turning back.
She says she cuts herself because
no one seems to care.
Sometimes she longs to tell someone,
but she doesn't dare.
Half the time I can't explain
what I say and do.
For all I know if I were her,
I'd cut myself too.
So, there is no judging her.
There is no need for shame.
She will not plead guilty,
for she's not the one to blame.
She bleeds out the hurt
when life gets too rough.
I wonder what will happen
when she cannot bleed enough.
When you keep on bleeding,
and the pain just consumes
you need to heal something
inside of you.
Put down the razor.
Put down the knife.
Don't let this kill you.
Take back your life.
And each day will be
better than before.
Until you wake up one day
and you bleed no more.

Over

The truth that bends.
The cold that burns.
Down to your sound,
smooth as your curves.
He was dark as night.
…hazel eyes…
Words come in
like the tide.
Should have been over,
but it had barely began.
I should have stood my ground,
but instead I ran.
Head thrown back,
the agony of defeat.
Right then and there
it should have been over for me.

The Location of the Heart

Where is the location
of the heart?
Cracks in time.
The same shape
as the cracks in the wall.
I never got around
to fix that leak.
You said it was
a nightmare.
But this is real.
I look for the details.
I wish I had
known you better.
But you knew me
at your best.
The glory of the garden.
Funny how it sounds
fine in your head.
Now I understand
what all the hate was for.
I want you to know
I'm not angry anymore.

Rocks

I move through the fear
Like the water through my hands
Emotions grip me
That I don't understand
It confuses the issue
The point is blurred
My mind is mangled
My eyes are disturbed
But I never believed
In matching my socks
I don't like smooth sand
I enjoy the rocks
That pierce my feet
Until they're bleeding and worn
But they thicken the skin
So it can't be torn

Song

I just need a fix
Just one more hit
One more time around
To prove I can make it
Things have gotten hard
But they could be worse
Like you know the song
But you forgot the verse
Like you found the map
But you lost the need
Like you have the lock
But you broke the key
Like you found your song
But it's been sung
Like you need to love
But you're just too numb

Devil's Due

I know you don't like me
And I guess that alright
I wish there was somewhere
I could stay for the night
Wrestling with your shadow
Devil's got his due
You know those lies I fed you?
Some of them were true

For Alex

What good is it to survive if
you are barely alive?
Too sick to live.
Too nauseated to turn your head.
Choking down your pills.
Losing your hair.
Too tired to get up.
Too tired to care.
Artificially alive and just
marking time.
Others clean up after you.
The air tastes like broken stone.
You don't know how to be alone.
A fancy name for a ghoul.
What good is a thorn-less rose?
Are you lying to me--
or just wrong?
You fooled everyone but yourself.
A cuckoo's egg; a deranged chemist--
gulp down another piece of raw flesh.
Put an ice pack on your head.
During the worst of it,
you sometimes hear your sister's voice.
But what you really needed was a choice.

Cancer In My Chest

I have cancer in my chest.
I tried to say it before, but the
words got stuck in my throat,
thick as molasses.
The cells are dividing
in the malignant stage and it
drains me. Though sometimes I
question what is really making
me so tired.
I don't fear cancer.
I fear the thoughts--
the goddamn thoughts it
leaves in my head.
Germs grow fast.
Cancer is faster.
It all looks so harmless on paper.
Like I can play it off
as a metaphor.
I hate my body for betraying me.
Every day you lose a little more.
Every day I'm
a little less free.
I tell you that I am okay,
as the cancer in my chest
is killing me.

Dripping With Sin

You cry from nightmares
That you invite in
You claim to be purest
When you're dripping with sin

Echo

It started as a joke that
I just made up.
Poison in the center.
But animals should be naked.
The hunger of the body—
a need to be close and pressed
against someone else.
I felt your loneliness.
I felt your need.
I felt it echo back from my eyes.
It's wrong to be near you and
not touch you.
I nod when I don't trust my voice.

Feel My Hunger

Your breath against my pulse
was soft and half-strangled with
needs you were fighting.
Your lips were heat
against my skin.
I already touched what I wanted to
taste and I wanted you.
I wanted you to
Feel my hunger.
You shuddered inside my mouth
as if you were breathing me—
as if you would crush me against you.
You wanted power and control:
To be the sober one around
broken people flocking around you.
You think it makes you stronger.
But it just makes you
twice as fucked up as they are.

Silver

Small children begin to disappear.
Fever pitch claim the result.
I taste silver, but who is
hunting who?
You attract evil like a moth to a flame.
I'd love to catch you awake—
Tear your shirt open.
The men on street corners know
some wounds never heal.
Take the keys from your jailor
who's too wounded.
I want you to handle it, but
the moon controls the tide.
Don't put up a struggle—
Throw your body to the jackals.
I can sense the danger and
your intentions.
I am not sick…
I am insane.
Wash me clean but
don't stop the game.

God Is Broken

You are beautiful nightmare.
There was a fire in your gut, though
you claimed to feel no pain.
I bought you this silver chalice
if you come to the ceremony.
Have something good to make up for.
I am so drug demented,
it drips off my skin and
it slithers away.
It poisons my mind as it
slides down the drain.
Pathetic little corpse.
I was choking on the wet silk
of my own terror.
The fear was the weight that
Slammed me to the floor.
Bright and burning and holy.
You were so proud of your wounds,
but your god is broken and
I cannot give you courage.

Trash

Here I am again staring---
trying to see straight.
It seems I have forgotten who to
Love and who to hate.
Always those voices get you
as you open the door.
Stare at dirty pictures, but she
doesn't want you anymore.
Here's to the ones I can't console.
And here's to the ones who know
it's fool's gold. Now you tell me,
what is a man?
Does he know when to quit, or
know when to bend?
There's blood in my mouth
from where your teeth have been.
There's blood in my mind
from the trash she's talking.
Don't bury me— I'm not dead yet.
I just can't remember what I should forget.
I suffered long before you spoke.
She says you can't fix what's not broke.
When she held me, it was much too tight.
I said, "I don't have long," but actually
I had all night.
You're just the stain
that never came clean.
You're just that asshole that
never saw me.
I am trying to break your heart,
but I can't finish what
you won't start.
I'm feeling pretty blank and
I have you to thank.
So, I try to do the math in my head.
I try to kick you out of my bed.
I'm so lonely, but
at least I'm not wrong.
This cancer I've invited
has eaten to the bone.

Radio

Hand the bottle over,
I need more wine.
Just one more fucked up
reason you are not mine.
But you don't seem to care
what's on, as long as it
lasts until dawn.
And you don't seem to care
if it's right, as long as you
kiss by moonlight.
No feelings at all.
The emotions are cold.
Every time they come close
they still misquote.
If it looks like a lie that
doesn't make it a lie.
And it doesn't mean I didn't
enjoy it at the time.
I could talk until I'm dead, but
never understand your head.
Crimson lines over your pale skin.
Hold me down, and
drive the nails in.
Sleep off the demons
that alcohol brings.
Pull me apart until I
rip at the seams.

Sweet Sickness

Would it please you that
I thought of his death?
Your gaze is like a fish hook
dragging across my skin.
You haven't shaved for weeks.
It's so hot I think I will catch fire.
You laugh like a child.
On a white tile floor, the
blood looks so loud.
It climbed right out of the ground.
You spread through me like
a sweet sickness.
You got out of rehab, and
went into denial.
That looks like me—the patchwork man.
Reopen my wounds with
false hope.
You're big enough to fuck me over, and
small enough to make me think
it was my idea.
You are a convincing mark, but
I have been this way since birth.

Monster

I upset all the right people.
You were looking for me, and
I was looking for you.
Drinking just turned me into
the same asshole you were.
The sun does not give off light:
It magnifies the dark.
I will make it possible.
When I break you,
I'll start with your thumbs.
Take this needle out of my arm.
Take the pain killer.
Feel it one last time.
There's violence in my head—
Not sexual, but comforting.
You are made of sharp edges, and
so painfully real.
The people you call your friends
do you so much harm.
You caught the monster, and now
you are the monster.
Lick your wounds, but
don't live in them.

MYTH:

One look in my eyes and you will openly deny everything you believe in.

Medusa

When you walk down my halls
you step in shit.
Such a malicious triumph.
Only the blind are safe.
I lost myself in despair,
but never quite learned to disappear.
Blood streams from my neck;
his weapon was a mirror.
The mirror found me,
I could not hide.
So utterly dismantled.
Poseidon's pride is a fragile thing.
I didn't want him inside me.
I could see his lies as easily as I
see my breath on the frozen air.
I cannot wash him off.
End my torment, Persus.
Kill this fragile heart.
They taught you how to be a hero.
Who is the monster now?
The mirror shows what I have become,
and you are as welcome
as the angel Gabriel.
Athena knew I had to be
deflowered before I was devoured, and
her twisted words turned my
world into a private hell.
Sometimes I talk to the statues here.
They won't tell my secrets.
Their tongues are stone.

Reynard

There's a cunning necessary for survival
A craft over brute strength
Nasty, but charismatic
I can talk my way out of anything
You must always question them
To question is to exist
I am the wisest fool
Trickery and deceit are my best defense
I'm the fox in your hen house
Do not accept things blindly
Through creation I sometimes destroy
as I point out the flaws in society

"Mighty Wand" Midgard

…………………I have fantasies
I include the Asir in them
Rending flesh
Blood-red violence
I will destroy anything in my path

 There's a hollowness inside me
I have no language
Just a terrible hunger and
the rage of my scales and fangs
I did not mind the water
it soothes the beast within
I grow larger and larger
burrowing into the ocean's bed

 They tell me I will
smash the skull of Thor
Ragnarok's rage is an
all consuming anger

Clever One

The Clever One said
I need to make room
Because something precious
Died too soon
I know he's not perfect
Neither am I
I know I can make it better
I hope you know I try
All of these struggles
Clouding my veins
I've paid for with blood
I broke through the pain
Some days will be torture
I welcome it
Maybe I am weak
For not giving a shit
I know it's not easy
Not much self-esteem remains
I've lost something precious
But just look what I've gained

Frigg

Weaving clouds and
the threads of fate
Queen of the Aesir
it's never too late
Marshy and boggy
was the sacred ground
Wisdom spinning without
a sound
The power of prophecy
ravens, hawks, and falcons
Yet I was unable
to save my own son
Marriage and childbirth
Wisdom and weaving
My hands will not slow
I never stop spinning

Tyr

I do not fear the wolf

A balanced nature and
a love for battle
I said it was I who
killed the child
It was a lie
My hand in the wolf's mouth
A tearing sound-- a snap--
a gasp of pain
A piece of me savagely ripped away
It's not like I never suffered
a wound before
Far deeper than the loss of a limb
A part of my identity
was ripped off

The wound refuses to heal

Odin

I carved the world
from the giant Ymir
after I killed him
I am the All Father
The High One
The Hanged God
Lord of the Gallows
One Eye
Gray Traveler
Bringer of Death
Eternal Wisdom
The World Shaker
The Giant Slayer
No one dares to question me
No one dares to stand up
I can see the future and the past yet
I am powerless to prevent it
Everlasting sorrow
You cannot hope to understand
They will never believe Loki, for I
have named him The Father of Lies
Ignorant pawns
I was old when mountains were new
None but I have seen
what is yet to be
Fate cannot be prevented
I let it happen
My own crimes will
be my undoing
I am the gods greatest enemy
The faces of the dead laugh at me

None can fathom my burden

Loki

Anger burns my thoughts
Pain haunts me from within
Deception is my specialty
Chaos is my friend

A head for revenge
Mixed with a genius mind
I tell my own truth
Yet I am the God of Lies

They say I am a parasite—
All I do is take
Yet every time they call on me
To cover their mistakes

Bound to this rock
Poison in my eyes
Covered in my son's dried blood
There's so much truth in lies

Without me lies peace
Within me lies change
How many others will have to suffer
So the gods can feel no pain

Sigyn

Here I stand above you
There is not much time left
Love, don't fulfill your destiny
Not all promises should be kept

I cling to the only one I knew
They call me the "faithful" one
Yet when they took you a part of me died
As they brutally slaughtered our son

Shielding your eyes from the poison
Shielding their eyes from the truth
My heart burns and your body shakes
As they poison the poison in you

I am dying with you
Shielding agony from your eyes
Holding back Ragnarok
Forever by your side

I'm confused by all your lies
But confused by their lies more
But, love, my arms are getting numb
And my hands are so sore

Hela

Ah, loneliness, a welcome friend.
I needed her to stay.
One side of me is beauty,
one side of me is decay.
I tower over the dead,
more terrifying than any monster
you create inside your head.
My father, the Hated One,
he gets no love from me.
He can stay bound for all I care—
crying to be free.
I was born of lust and hate;
the youngest of the three.
The damned come to my door
forever drawn to me.
All I feel is jealousy,
hatred, grief, and pain.
My father meant to redeem me,
but I'm damned just the same.

Fenris

When I was born my father knew
that I would be the one.
He taught me how to be cruel;
I am the faithful son.
The gods can try to capture me,
but I don't think they can.
I made a deal with Tyr, and
I took off his hand.
I feel almost a wolf, but
never quite a man.
The gods want to capture me,
I'm pretty sure they can.
My father came to me one day and
placed his hand on my head.
He told e Ragnarok would come—
soon they will be dead.
I stay on my cold island,
not knowing how to flee.
I pray and wait for the dawn of time
to see if gods can bleed.

ARES

Fighting in a war
Doesn't make you a believer.
I love the battle for its own sake.
My nature is savage and
OVERWHELMING.
Many hate a dangerous force.
SLASH THE SHEEP!
A MILLION SHADES OF EMOTION.
WICKED NIGHT DELIGHT.
TERRIBLE DARK FRENZY.
It's the battle within
I could never understand.
Sometimes the right thing to do...
is the wrong thing

Hephaestus

With all these ghosts
we'd be lost--
but the sun is still coming up.
I am bent over my anvil,
hard at work on a metal creation.
When I was young,
I only thought of getting numb.
A thousand years of night.
Darkness all around me;
crazed by mercury.
"I have no mother."
Lame as the result of
my greatest fall.
I have the urge within me to
slice something up.
This arsenic exposure
cast me out of "heaven"
where only the devils belong.

Heimdall

Ever watchful sentinel;
the strong and silent type.
The Gjallar horn waits for your call
as you protect them with your life.
Can you hear the green grass grow,
and see a hundred leagues?
I see you on the Bifrost bridge
drinking the finest mead.
Heimdall, the whitest of the gods
keep watch for Ragnarok.
Your foreknowledge is a blessing and a curse;
a puzzle you can not unlock.
You carry the weight of the world on your back,
loyal to the end.
You will obey the All-Father;
you will protect them.

Wolf Son

I have grown strong here;
I am a danger to all.
A terrible blend of a wolf and a man;
I want what we all want.
I want to know where I come from.
They killed my father and sister.
I was cast out in the forest.
The exiled one is my father.
What do you know of peace, you
who murder infants?
He took all from me.
My agony is constant.
Blade in my maw—
rusty as my cage.
And all I can feel
is an all-consuming rage.

Somatic Tremor

It's a somatic tremor.
I know it has to be
The midgard serpent.
Destroyer of worlds and
savior of us all.
Easy bruising and
night sweats—
unexplained fevers.
There's a wild creature
in my eye.
You say you like what you see?
I was reborn in your wilderness.
Captivity set me free.
I would cross the street
to avoid myself.
It's always the insomniacs
that sleep around.
It isn't the dead we cry for.
We cry for the living, so
why waste your pity on me?

Trickster

The snake coils
Around my black heart
Your mistletoe twig
In the shape of a dart
A trickster; a liar
You are the clever on
An assassin for hire
With hair like the sun
I never knew darkness
As intimate as now
His face like an angel
But his language foul
They screamed at this ice child
To hold his tongue
His jokes press too far
Until they bitterly stung
Every creature he creates
Is a hideous being
Because the fire sprite thinks
He is ugly
Never boring or dull
Never quite sane
On his face sits a smirk
To cover the pain

Master of Fear

I always wanted to fit in.
But something inside me... is wrong.
I will not return to that decay.
I no longer worship in that
Temple of Suffering.
There's a thunder of a heartbeat in my ears.
The prey recognizes the predator.
A whisper against the strain
of a garbage bag.
The butcher block makes me forget
what my hands are there for.
His eyes-- showing too much white.
The fear grows and
so does the joy.
This is who I am.
One look in my eyes
and you will openly deny
everything you believe in.

The Riddler

A bowler hat
A green suit
A domino mask and
complex clues

Smooth talking
Yet quite quirky
I delight in
the forewarning

My father was a drinker
The constant rejection
made me want to prove
my innocence of deception

Out of jealousy
I was beaten and abused
My compulsion was born
out of desire for truth

I am superior
A narcissist
I must always prove
I am the best

I will show Gotham
how I can shine
But the riddling is lost
to the rhyme

Without a riddle
there is no crime
I didn't even want to leave
any clues this time

My enormous ego
is really to blame
And a deep rooted fear
I might be insane

Two Face

Acid in my face
Duality and fate
Because of bipolar disorder
(No. Schizophrenia.)
and a history of child abuse
We can all find a reason and then
sometimes become that reason
Good or evil is based
on the flip of a coin

And I have the scars to prove it.

Taskmaster

I don't trust my memory
Memories will fool you
They parade themselves around like facts
but are much too neon and garish
The best things I have ever done
are lies

But I am getting ahead of myself

I saw off the barrel of my gun
and take credit for my innocence
The shadow initiative can cover almost anything

Too late I realize I am Icarus
and the wax is melting faster
What little I remember of my childhood
is not people or places, but things
Water, and thicker wet things sliding down
my throat—no air, no air—and the choking

There is a monster in this void
With the face of a skull
It takes a moment to recognize the mirror

I knew I could teach them
and my students call me "master"
But there is nothing inside me
that isn't stolen

I am one thing made of many things
and each skill rips me through
But how do you correct a problem
when the problem is obviously you?

Madrox

Does it bother you when
life makes no sense?
So many personalities
yet I am still lonely.
I absorb more memories, but
I can't steal feelings
and I feel a little less each day.
We are filled with blood,
the challenge is to keep it inside.
I crave being the center of attention.
My jokes hide my pain.
How can a simple man be so complicated?
Motown music and noir films;
I search for clues to find myself.
Now I wash away the tight misery
of trying to be someone I was never meant to be.

MEPHISTO

I RULE A FIERY REALM--
EMPOWERED BY THE SOULS OF THE DAMNED
SOME CALL ME DEVIL, SOME CALL ME SATAN--
IT DOES NOT MATTER WHO I AM
IF YOU ARE EXTREMELY POWERFUL
EXCEPTIONALLY PURE AND TRUE
ONE WAY OR ANOTHER
MEPHISTO WILL GET TO YOU
THERE IS NO FAITH AND LOVE
NO HATE AND MISERY
IN THE END YOU WILL ALL BE GONE
ALL THAT WILL BE LEFT IS ME
EVERYTHING WILL DIE
WHEN YOUR DEATH TAKES ITS TOLL
I SHALL DO EVERYTHING I CAN
TO POSSES YOUR SOUL
IT DOES NOT MATTER WHAT YOU DO
IT DOES NOT MATTER WHAT YOU SAY
STRIKE A BARGAIN WITH ME...
SOONER OR LATER WE ALL HAVE TO PAY

Iron Man

For every heaven
there is a hell.
For every dream--
a nightmare.
For every beautiful thing---
a swift kick in the teeth.

This suit protects me
as I protect the world:
shrapnel moving towards my heart.

 I never could relate to people.

One part playboy,
one part scientist,
one part hero.
Yet, the pieces didn't quite fit together.
Most of this wealth was inherited
by a tragic accident.
You tell me, was it worth it?
Yet, out of all the monsters I have faced
alcohol was the strongest--
slipping into the tiniest cracks.
It's hard to move ahead when you are
constantly looking over your shoulder.
But I always enjoyed being a disappointment
to thugs in authority.

This gift is a curse.

Havok

I never wanted to be a hero.
But I guess you can get used to anything.
Even an orphanage, or
floating in a limbo-like void.
I absorb and transform
cosmic radiation.
But I'm more interested in geophysics.
I could never be as good as Scott
anyway, so why try?
I thought I would be so much
better than I am by now.
I can't stand the thought of
seeing the disappointment
reflecting from their eyes.
Perhaps I don't care about your opinion.
Or maybe I never asked you
because I am terrified of the answer.

Rictor

You have no idea how it feels
to be so connected to the earth that
you feel every whisper and tremor.
They say it's earthquake generation.
Powerful waves of vibrations
causing your world to shatter around you.
Like mine was shattered when it was all taken away.
Now a piece of me is missing and I
can't fill the empty space.
There's not enough room inside me for the pain.
Powerless detective.

I was never very good at loving women.
But when my eyes met his
everything clicked into place and I knew
exactly who I am.
I may be a queer hero, but
this little homo can kick your ass.

It shouldn't matter anyway.
The point in the end is
to love the people around you
the best that you can.

Copycat

The difference between magic and power
is very small.
I become attached too easily.
And it rains, and I bleed; I'll
be who you want me to be.

But there is this fear-- what will
he do if I say stop?

Will he stop?

 Impersonation will gain trust,
you shape-shifter, how easily you
fall in love and lose track of the mission.
Mental imprints.
Plastic love always paid well.
But I am only as cold as the
darkness made me.

King Lycan

King Lycan served Zeus
human flesh.
For this he was punished.
Psychiatric wards.
A taste of doom.
Devoured by the next full moon.
Be it curse or bite—
sometimes you're born with it.
Crocodiles carry the souls of
murder victims yearning for revenge.
Torment my spirit.
Demons are the ultimate
shape-shifters.
Wodan was the god of ecstasy—
Old Norse Fury.
Insensitive to fire and pain---
they never bleed.
You are either too smart, or too dumb
to believe in a god.

Lamias

Skoll will devour the sun
Hati will devour the moon
The incubus is a jealous lover
One look will make you impotent but
Needs must when the devil drives
I pick things over people
You can fix things when they break
I use my body when my mind is a mess
Why do the ones you aren't really your friends
Insist on baring their souls
Wipe your hands
This great hulking thing is
Dodging cars and hiding behind bushes
Lamias stay in the shadows
Your face is horribly distorted
Your skin seems to be on fire
You always had a way with words
Silvanus hides like a wolf in the woods
If you kill someone, you kill a part of yourself
I would leave you in a hole
In the desert

Beat of Wings

Feed pound
into the ground
Purposely lost
to be found
Hazy night
Beat of wings
Insect laughter
Jagged teeth
Razor claws
Beat of wings
Forked tongue
Bat squeak
Face pressed
into the ground
Heaven's child
Hell bound

Hunt the Whore

Hunt the whore
Broken teeth
Hideously real
Light my cigarette
I think I am ugly
Madness rattles the flesh
Bare your bones
My body throbs
Teach me how to ride
Bent slightly
Drag me down
Smoke these limbs
Dangling daisies
I will not forgive you
Fondle my music
It comes in waves
Grinning blank eyes roll up
Skull hacked open
Feel what was lost
Corrupt the confusion
Blankness brings thieves
Through my tired veins
Silence screams

Killian

When he came in
the pressure in the air felt
like a storm gathering.
Just a look will make you
howl in hysteria.
His bad reputation protects
him more than magic.
He is the pain that shocks you from sleep,
"cancer" and "poison" on your lips.
The world kneels before him
following every whim.
He is as beautiful as a
sculpture of razor blades.
And just as deadly.

Drunk With A Gun

If a person can fold
1,000 cranes
they will be granted one wish
Sea turtles die
on the same beach they were born
Mutations are genetic anomalies
Ignorance creates monsters and there's
nothing sadder than a con man conning himself
With just one bullet you
could be a hero
I'm a drunk with a gun
It took away the fear
If you grow up in pain it
becomes a part of you
You make my chest hurt
Go ahead and accuse me
I have to keep myself
Put the knife under your pillow
Paint me a future
Lives trapped in paint
Monsters struggling to survive
And then you start screaming

Churning

I woke up too early
Blood dried on my hand
My world spun around me
When I tried to take a stand
The bile in my belly
Casts a fire in my eyes
I smoke to ward off demons
Who never compromise
Struggle to stay awake
As my blurry vision clears
Press my forehead to the pillow
To calm these churning fears

Knees

A howl erupts
From inside the dark
Sometimes it is over
Before it can start
The fog covers
Body; hands
Feet pound the pavement
Fast as they can
Hiss from a shadow
Road never ends
It grows like fear
Dark and twisted
Surrounded by eyes
A silent scream
With a bitter cry
Fall to your knees

ETHAN:

That doesn't make me crazy. Just lonely.

Chew Your Tongue Out

You would have thought it was a bad idea
Nuts to that
Finally, you said,
sign me up
Lord only knows what you were seeing
I have another stupid question
Chew your tongue out
You send a psychopath to stop a psycho
The feeling was tremendous
Death was always the punch line
We could all see it coming
I just want it to stop bleeding
Surrender your conscience
And I felt robbed
Does it get worse than this
Not everything about being human is nice
You were a crease in the cloth
It's just tricks
You try to keep me scared because
you can't actually DO anything
We send the victim to do the right thing
What's bliss for me is
torture for you
There's a difference in staying alive
and in living

Again

I have ginseng in
My blood stream
Freezing my flame
The servant of
The foam sting
The day that he came

I have bitter orange
White willow seed
Spark turns to sand
Ginger melts into caffeine
Dust in my hand

Never feeling that
Never feeling that again

Sex Change

In the afterlife
Reptile-like smile
I can deal with your brand of pain
If it will erase the thoughts in my brain
When did I become the enemy?
Am I even human anymore
Or an animal—a great aching
Need that never quite gets released
It is always inside you and you
Never know when it might strike
How can you be the first to finish
When you're the last to start?
You penetrate me with your eyes
And you're weak from staying
On your knees
There's blood on the flowers
You can almost taste your own release

But you have to live with the body you have

Truth

Things are getting dangerous
I twist around your vine
Wading through circumstance
Absorbing all my time
It's a delicious thought
It's my newest sin
I told myself I wouldn't
But I always give in
I willingly burn
As I wait for your hand
Words that knock me over
Cut me down where I stand
Tell me the truth
Blind me to see
I cover your body
I accept the sting
Tell me the truth
Crying to be
Just whatever you do
Don't fucking lie to me

Wings

A charge of treason
you defended your arrogance
fighting against the very god who saved you
They will scream "traitor"
just to hear their voices break
against the walls like fine china
Evil has set up home here
Your silence is caged and beating
within your heart with the fury
of leather-like wings
He tries not to tell the truth in public
God revels in the white lies
God—or something else
Old enemies feel like family--
they know you better than anyone else
His brutality is casual
His eyes gleam with excitement—
wicked thoughts squirming in his mind
I don't understand why you don't run away
Old age doesn't slow him down--
it just makes him sneakier
His gift is getting answers
No one can say no to him
He is ruthlessly charming
I always thought he would make
a really good vulture

Pounds of Flesh

I saw you the night you
ransacked the church.
You stole pounds of flesh
from skeletons dry as
bones. You kissed me like
a drowning man. Your face
filled my sky, and your
beauty blurred my mirror.
I will clean your wounds
with my tongue. You hide
an angel behind your eyes.
Flowers grow out of your
skull. The edge to your
voice was filled with
such anger. It made
me love you.
I write you love letters
when no one is
looking. With no
witness I can pretend you
aren't real. Feelings come and
go like white static, and the
only constant thing is my life is
my heart beat.
Even that wants to get away from
me, it seems. There is too much
blame here and I can't
breathe with it crushing my
chest. A handful of dust. A
forgotten dream. You are
brilliant from too much poison.
Predictably irrational.

Blood Sacrifice

I held on so fiercely that my hand
ached to what I never had in the
first place
I cannot forgot who I am
I cannot forget your fingers
It stays with me, like the sweet smell
of blackening flesh peeling back
Rooks cry in wild fury
Your havoc has turned tragic
Your pain is not in season
My mouth is raw and
my veins stalk me down
My thighs are ambushed
by the speed of your eyes
There's a sharp pain of doubt—
it resides in me
You are a clever demon and
violent in your need
They shot the animal in me and
the animal in me screams
Sew up my bleeding wound
If I don't die soon— I might get killed
I'm drawn to the warmth in you
It was a light I always worshipped
You think through your cock
Soft as a prayer
Power is blood sacrifice
It was the wrong kind of excitement:
an animal wanting to be fed
I can feel it gathering,
throbbing in my pulse
"This will not hurt," you said, and your
voice promised more painful
things to come.

Sigman Road

Check out this crazy fucker--
shaking paws, he left me his card
on the corner of Sigman Road.
I am stuffing surgical gloves into my
purse to use as balloons later.
His tone was quiet and cold.
My stomach hurts because
I am trying not to laugh.
I swallowed the evidence—
bitter taste in my mouth.
I remember the trail of blood
littering the floor to my door.
It seems that sociopaths travel in packs.
The trees block the sun here.
Your candy tastes like violence.
It will shock you how much it
never happened.
You can't stand on your feet,
and I can't do it for you.
I can't flap your wings
without losing my focus.
Honesty is not the point because
there is no truth.
You are dangerous because
you know you are right.

Real Nightmare

His mouth tightened and I knew
I'd said the perfectly wrong thing.
The day had been a monster.
The lack of oxygen kept him down.
The pressure in the thoracic cavity
seemed to knit over his wounds.
One piece and a thousand fragments.
I am a wild creature that has broken from
its cage and mutilated its keeper.
Like a nightmare, it seemed that
I had always been running.
A wounded animal too stubborn to die.
Bones would crack in shards and splinters,
as he spoke in a voice like a burning orphanage.
He looked like the kind of guy
who promises the first hit is free.
Smile bright with a terrible rage.
I saw what I feared most in his eyes.
No one can bear to face a real nightmare
when it is standing before them.

The Dead Still Bleed

There are things that will hate you
just for being what you are.
The razor burns a line
almost resembling a smile.
I've become very good at
not looking back.
His voice was like a spider
crawling down my neck.
And now my mind is swerving
into the blackest evening.
The different between insanity and
sadism doesn't matter a lot
to the victim.
If one doesn't answer just move to the other.
It's better than letting the beast out.
My control rattles in its cage.
It's here that I finally feel my age.
Sometimes the dead still bleed.
Sometimes the thing that will save you
will also trap you.
It's very hard being a survivor;
sometimes you have to believe in magic.
Perhaps I am the bad guy;
depends on how you look at it.
You know everything about me,
except for where I hide.
There's always more to cover up
the truth within a lie.

Hateful Eyes

His face is heavy lined
Life has cut into him
Mocking grin that said the world is
Insane and he knows why
Eyes that look through you--
You're just in the way
He won't lose his focus
He brings stark terror by
The fistfuls
Murder in his veins
Your own desire startles you
I have found the part of you that
I like the most
The danger is never in the dying

A snake in wolf's clothing
He hates you with all of his parts
He sees butter as a weakness
He needs more than change in his
Broken cup—the kind of justice where
You hate your opponent
You just get lost in those hateful eyes

Boiling Alive

Stay focused;
the operation is about to begin.
You aren't healing right.
It's taking far too long.
The heat comes from within,
as though I am boiling alive
from the inside out.
I feel I could breathe fire like a
dragon if I wanted to.
My touch could melt a glacier.
These scars are all wrong.
They tell too much.

Canopy of Tears

Beneath a canopy of tears,
I fucked another man.
It was the first time
the world seemed to shift, as the
guilt mixed with the lust.
Who made me this way?
My cock seemed to burn and
my hands moved without my consent.
He whispered things to me that
I didn't realize I wanted to hear.
He possessed me & owned me.
The shift of control was sublime.
How can it be a sin, this love?
How can it be anything but sacred?
A man touching another man,
as only another man can.

Umbrella

The rain pounded, and
the umbrella didn't stand a chance.
I'll get right to the point.
Sometimes you have to fall to rock
bottom before you can rise again.
It was my pretty poison.
The sting that feels so sweet.
I'm a fool for a felon.
I tremble and it's garish; I am
paralyzed by the truth.
This is the part where we kiss.
There's no such thing as small change.
Even people you don't like die.
I'll slip a note under your door.
If you can keep the bullets out of
your gun, I'd offer you a reaction.
Sometimes I fear a part of you has
escaped and been passed onto me.
I look in the mirror and
suddenly see your eyes.
Maybe I was made for rescuing you.

What the Body Does

She gave me a dose of white noise.
You should be more careful of
the stories you put yourself in.
It's so much easier to think of you not like me.
Sometimes it takes almost dying
to really appreciate what your body does.
Breathing is suddenly a miracle, and
you study your own fingerprints in wonder.
I'm too sane to sit here
shuddering—rotting and forgotten while
they frolic in the sun.

Unattainable

I am in love and powerless.
I have the horrible urge to abandon you.
You see, I thought I was saving you…
But I was naive.
It was you who saved me, and
I cannot give you back.
The women flock to you like delicate birds.
And you cradle each one—
always surprised and overwhelmed that
they would want you.
They want to rescue you because
you are beautiful.
Because you are unattainable,
and gentle,
and awkward,
and you curse yourself for
your own lack of control.

Gloves in the Rain

You won't be the last person dead of AIDS.
You certainly weren't the first.
Just the first I knew.
And don't get me wrong, dear,
I hurt for them too.
But sometimes it feels like it's
me that is dying.
You have given me so much strength.
You taught me gratitude, and
you taught me to believe.
You ask me for more morphine, and
I stare at all the pills.
I want so much to hold you, but
I know I never will.
I shield myself from AIDS,
like I have been taught to do.
I wear gloves in the rain, and
I am a stranger to you.
It's dangerous—the way we talk.
You say kissing is not possible,
because it makes your lungs ache
with the need to breathe.
I want so much for you to live.

Pride

You wear your hatred out in the open.
Smokey memories bleed.
I am a ghost slammed against a wall—
I can't remember anything.
I loved your sharp edges the most.
The crows tell me many things,
like murder in my head.
I talk to people no one else can see.
That doesn't make me crazy.
Just lonely.
Nothing makes sense in silence.
I feel the darkness like an ache
low—very low in my gut.
You shudder with ecstasy and
drink me like a mystery.
Justice got her eyes cut out
by ignorance and pride.
The caves they left festered and bled—
they barely resembled eyes.
Without me you would die.
I want to hide the ugly truth.
Then no one would ever know
I think I am better than you.

Already Broken

You can't break
what's already broken.
God will pick up
where the medicine leaves off.
If you knew where to find him.
Well, I must be the crazy one.
I just need one more night
to prove the bastard right.
I looked god in the eye
until god looked away.
The stars were cold.

Fists Like Bullets

No one saw anything
because that is the rule.
My pulse is in my throat as
I breathe through your mask.
Strip me down to my bones
as the terror sets in.
Don't ask me why I can't
leave without my heart and
I won't ask how you can.
You trust so quickly
when they say they believe in you.
And you lived your life like a flower,
always catching the rain.
You would never hurt anyone, yet
you died in pain.
You've got nothing else to do so
you starved me on silence
with fists like bullets.

Monster Mirror

I hear my thoughts
in your silence
The stars are scattered
but it's not the moon's fault
Bend me down with sin
There is no proof and
I can't believe the
animal in me will leave me be
I want you to know who
slipped the blade in slow
Do any of you really give a shit?
The importance of time management
You lack the passion and
there is nothing more chaotic
than the beat of a heart
It warms my chambers
This is not life
It is sickness
Pull yourself together
Lightening bugs lead me home
The monster in me
can't see
the monster in the mirror
Even you would do vile things
for the greater good

Invade

The angel screaming in my head
woke up the devil
My blood was shaking and
so were my hands
I traded my story for your dark and
I stayed to let it invade
I took the light in and could hear you
laugh in the wind
The angel screamed in my throat
The skin so blue as the walls
begin to sigh
My mind was gone and so were you
I have been running most of my life
Peel my wounds back in defeat
What if I was wrong and everyone
else was right
I can't hide behind the drugs
Drinking your life down will
shake the devil up
Laughter in my ear
There was no place to go
Running down broken glass
Drain my life as you pump away

Worth Living For

No one has taken a bath recently.

Maybe I'll just go to China--
stay home and play with myself.
Are you done with that one?
I think it was a snapshot.
I felt like I couldn't
breathe anymore.
It can't be much further.

Did you take the ones
in the other room?
I don't do that anymore.

There's always something
worth living for.

Flesh Eater

This thing within me
That eats me alive
It takes away everything
My last breath of life
Its sharp little teeth
Dig into my flesh
It gets more and more
While I feel less and less
A horrible feeling
Of losing control
My mind is reeling
From the pain of the blow
And it slithers around
In my belly all the time
I know it hears me
As I slowly lose my mind
I know it feels the anguish
Of each sweat drenched night
As I scream out in terror
My skin sickly white
I can feel it grinning
In its blood soaked haven
And I have nothing inside
Left to be saving
So I trudge through the day
This thing moving inside
And I hear it laughing
Loud and clear in my mind

Vulture

The man who asked how
long I have to live
looked like a vulture.
It hurts... somewhere
deep in my chest, and I
feel that razor-edged
sadness that really only
comes with time. You
cannot read the future
by the lines in your
palm, but the past is
written there quite
clearly in our scars.
His eyes held an invitation,
but it wasn't to anything
pleasant. It was closer
to murder than to love.
I could tell by the
animal in his voice.
And just when I needed
To cherish my own
illusion.

Drink

Homosexual sadist
Even Hitler loved wolves
Poisoned by wolfsbane
Unwilling to die
Go to the slaughter
My spiritual double
The quality is so pure
You couldn't stop if you wanted to
I'll burn this room to the ground
A disaster so bad you can't
Lie to yourself anymore
It's so easy to fall off the edge

There are two types of men in the world
Some pour and some drink

I'll pour you a drink

COPPER

Hello.
You are at my place.
What happened to you?
I am good with secrets and
you have a reputation.
Cynicism is contagious.
Teeth gnawing on my instincts.
"If" is such a harsh word.
You've got nowhere to go.
No more half-measures.
There was so much blood, you
could taste it in the air.
Copper.

Lazarus

Dagger feelings through my mind.
I have a kinky preoccupation.
I have learned a lot from you.
Lupericus inspires you as
an insane butcher.
A grotesque and twisted terror.
The ground beneath my feet is solid.
Inhale all the scents.
Fear tastes metallic and salty.
Sweat in my mouth.
Desire tastes like fire and juniper.
A vanilla dream.

There is nothing I can do.
I can't turn.
This parasite within me
bleeds over with desperation.
I feel it in my bones.
I smell my own guilt.
All it takes it a lapse in judgment.
A delicate balance of
tight-rope walking.
Lazarus—it is the worst betrayal
not being able to control your body.
My skin itches and it wants to
peel back from my flesh
to show you what is underneath.
An unbearable heat from within.
Run your nails down my wall.
Murder this pain.

Band-Aids

She comes in like the breeze
Band-Aids on her knees
A warm and pleasing certainty
That she is perfect to me
She changes on a whim…

..she slips through my hands

Door

There he stood
at my door,
covered in blood;
in blisters and sores.
And what can you offer
such a being filled with pain?
Consumed by insanity;
infested with shame.
I sat up all night
talking in rhymes.
I almost reached him,
but ran out of time.
I fold my arms and
tightly clutch myself.
No one has to tell me
this will hurt like hell.

Sparks in a Land Mine

In darkness I move closer
to you, searching for your body heat--
needing your warmth, for my body is
ice and it flows through my veins.
I want your hands to roam
across my body, leaving embers behind.
Sparks in a land mine—
there is no safe way through.
You thought you had escaped but,
you were tricked into it.
Virgins do no interest me.
I want to blaze between your legs.
With greed I pull you down;
with lust to mold yourself against me.
With love I share my pulse.
I have become obsessed with
touching you— feeling your penis
grow hard--- like velvet under my fingers.
I have so little to offer and
even less to lose.
Nothing lasts but my desire
to see you again.
A mirage broken—
yet pulling me in.

Melt the Ice

Trapped in this room
Can't find the door
Can't help the feeling
I've been here before
It shocks my head
It bruises my brain
I thought I'd be different
But I'm still the same
I thought I'd be stronger
But I haven't changed
The trembling inside
Somehow remained
And it feels cold as death
This pain from within
I want to melt the ice
And start living again

Compound Fracture

There are things about me that are
strange. Cold. Deadly.
I can't numb the pain.
It will never heal right,
this compound fracture
given to you by your rapist.
You remember him every time
the air is freezing cold and wet.
It hurts.
It hurts like hell.
These shades of shame--
the color of our dreams—
the ink of our mind.
Your drugs taste like pepper.
Sliding gifts under doors.
Just because it isn't real doesn't
mean it can't hurt you.
There's a dark part of me that
holds an animal.
I need that wild part of you.
I may as well have gone blind
for what you did.
The rest of the world is
in black and white and you
are in color.

No Cure

The mind works hard to make sense of
a traumatic event.
There is no cure because
this is not a disease.
It hurts within being in this skin.
The thorns opened up wounds that
were too cold to feel.
Their eyes were black.
Nature is our teacher, but
I am safe here.
Outside the monsters hunt,
tasting the warm flutter of your pulse.
I just got darker as wounded predators do.
The smile melted from her face and
flowed unto yours.
When your skin tears, it
grows back tougher.
Blasphemies tumble, sharp pointed briars
glide through my brambles.
The blood under my skin is furious.
You search and you slice and you
put an end to this life.

Blink

You are only as sick as your secrets
This is not what I do
I don't understand it all
But I understand enough
What good is an unloaded gun?
You do what I say
If you let me I can help you
An invisible mouth
before the flood
Did I say that or think it?
Pain feeds pain
What's with that strange laugh?
Shade the truth
Does it make you feel better?
Or does it break you?
The least you could do is speak
I don't want you to remember time
I want you to forget it
Things are hard enough
without adding guilt
The colors fade from your eyes
But you never blink

TOURNIQUET:

Just skip the parts you don't like.

Intuition

He keeps to the shadows,
aware of every move.
She is a welcome challenge.
He will make her pay;
Intuition sounding off.
He will make her pay
in blood.
Metal sinking into flesh.
She feels the burn of the razor.
You can scream if you want to.
The pain blazes through
her body strangled by her cry.
There is nothing in his eyes
but static.
Her eyes go vacant and he feels
the rush.
The graves tremble in the sunlight,
and the old man taps his cane
in a rhythm only he knows.
Yet, my body goes with it.
I am smitten by your smile.
But your eyes are all wrong.
And like a weary animal, it seems,
you've come home to die.
But I don't think freedom can be won
staring down the barrel of a gun.
Dying for a cause doesn't make it yours.

Outcasts

Outcasts make their own rules.
I feel a throb somewhere in my throat.
The heart can so easily relocate itself.
I am not ready to become confetti.
It eats you alive.
You're poisoned to survive.
I will know how hard you try
by the deadness in your eyes.
You're cutting your nose to
spite your face. I guess I was
lucky, now that it's gone,
I can do what I please.
Iron in the blood.
Against the worst of odds,
she led me through
to drown in your faith.
I left you in shambles
and god is gone.
Because of me, you have to skulk.
But you always knew how to drown.
You asked me to stay awhile,
voice soft and thick, with an edge of whine.
If you don't do it willingly
there are always other options.
You are my favorite nightmare.
Life didn't just take you--
It stole my ability to heal you:
breathe you back to life.

fausse couche

I saw you out of the window
testing my car engine, though I
told you it was fine.
"What an asshole," I thought. But
I wanted to take it back when
you leaned into the car,
so weak your knees buckled,
and put your hand over your face.

So I'm the asshole.

You set off my flight-or-fight response.
(I always chose flight)
I was afraid of losing my balance.
But I am a creature in need.
Sometimes we make our own mirrors.
My grass is hungry in your ruins:
Hungry for your veins.
Rip me through and gnaw me to dust.
Eating flesh does not breed them for slaughter.
Footfalls on the sidewalk.
I am your prisoner, your creature.
My womb is dry and empty, and
there is less life in me.
Just another stone under the bridge.
Like refusing to give it a name
means it doesn't exist.
Rip through—my heart bled with the moon.
I feel them touching me with ghost
hands, but I am a desert drowning
in a two foot long coffin.

Komodo Dragon

Passed down through blood.
It's a necessary evil.
Give him a steely look.
Hunt me down like some
animal.
When he kisses me
I no longer flinch.
But some part of me is
crawled up inside
screaming murder.
No one wants to know
what you're really thinking.
Mouth teeming with bacteria.
After the teeth sink in, it will
track you, it's prey, for
hours--- even days--- until
the poison takes over and
you are helpless. Then
it eats you alive.

I don't belong, I just
pass through.

Shock Therapy

I always remember
those first two lines.
At least it's not shock therapy.
It's like you've done something
and you can't wash it off.
Every birth is another disaster.
But let my breath be your breath.
If a tiger knows it's strength,
no man can hold him down.
Alcoholics can drink until they are sick, or
dead, but never until they are satisfied.
Your brother tried to punish you, but he
wanted to become you.
The devil inside you wants you paralyzed.
If you reach for what's inside,
it is suddenly outside.
Here, you say, you touched my heart.
And, here, you say, you touched my soul.
I have been made vulnerable.
No longer protected by bones and flesh.
I could feel you reaching in.
Your silence tastes of muffled hysteria.
Take your grin and walk on home.

Thick Wet Things

Sparking black storms.
Your face was sinking
in horrible animation.
You're nothing more than a
smile that ends in blood.
Teeth filed down to points.
Clothes hanging in tatters with the
indifference of a scarecrow.
The best cure for shock
is shock treatment.
I choke on the cobwebs
as your voice crawls in my ear.
It was a bit like standing
in a dead animal,
surrounded by darkness and
thick wet things.
The smell hit me first and
it was difficult to breathe.
The ground sucks my feet.
Your arrows are easy to track
across streams and through thickets.
The dew fills my mouth until I break
open in a shimmer of echoes.
They always burn in glory.
Conceal the confusion.
I never doubted your ability to maim.
Rain down your rosary on me.
I sew on your broken wings, but
shadows taste of ash and pomegranates.
My narcisstic delirium has
turned to smoke in the wind.
I can't separate you from your shadow.

England

When I dream of England
I always see your face
True love leaves no bruises
that you can ever trace
The trees reach for the sky
This is my chance to feel human
And you should pass me by
My insides are thick with frost
My heart has no home
But I dream of England
On my throne of clean white bones
I'll teach you how to beg
It feels like gargling razor blades
Your opinions aren't worth
A drop of water in hell
It eats into you like a lie
A planted thought in your head

I could destroy you with a sneeze

Protection

Mother, don't worry about me
I sometimes walk the dark streets
But if I smell him in the breeze
I have a switchblade up my sleeve

Humility

Filled with love and humility
I nuzzle your palm
I dissolve in your pleasure
I smear along your sky
I kneel at your alter
Crammed full of faith
and sobbing my heart out
Your feet were so careless
It only takes one kiss
to betray yourself
Would you trail your smoke
Would you shriek and swing
Germans don't joke
Get your pride off the table
and cut your ego down to size
It would be a lie to say
I had no regret
An egomaniac with
an inferiority complex

Minor Miracle

She was the kind of pet people wanted.
Jut skips the parts you don't like.
The heart is powered by
electrical impulses.
To you I simply shrug.
There is nothing more dangerous than
a familiar face.
There is nothing special about my failure.
It is painful because it's so ordinary.
There's no passion in your judgment, so
I feed you scraps of sorrow.
You sound like a crow without hope.
I see my reflection in your scales, and
wait for a minor miracle.

Trunk

He's sleeping soundly
As I toss and turn
My mind's gone cold
But my face still burns
Now I will drive home
Pissed and drunk
A baseball bat
Ready in the trunk

Pulse

I cross out the days
as they drag by.
I promised to quit.
I promised to try.
For a while I thought
that I wouldn't make it.
But if it's not real
why should you fake it?
I want to be comfortable
in my own skin.
I want to become
your pulse from within.
I will breathe with you and
inhale your life
All of these cracks
will be mended tonight.
Your touch is magic.
If only you knew.
I don't want the others.
I only want you.

Somehow with you
I don't feel the hurt that
has been burning for so long.
Somehow with you
I fought through the fog and
came out feeling strong.
When I'm with you
feelings rush over
me like a tidal wave.
When I'm with you
this little coward has
somehow become brave.

Nightmare

My eyes snapped open
Sickness filled my head
Agony in my stomach
No blood between my legs
From inside my body
I felt it kicking me
Something doesn't belong here
Sometimes I think it's me
He waits outside the door
And I sit on the cliff
Relying on devices
Two stripes on my strip
He takes my hand and clasps it
I pour out the wine
He laughed and smiled at me
But it did not reach his eyes

Shark

Silent as a shark
You sneak behind her
Cold and intense
Blinding white terror
Impersonal and cracked
Mirror for the predatory
Insect laughter
Like a bat's squeak
Searing memories
In no shape or form
Lips like daggers
Hands like thorns
She must endure this
How much longer
In his eyes burned
A horrible hunger

Twisted Time

I feel no need
To beg or plead
I feel no desire
To explain my spire
I need to cry
I need to feed
In order to survive
I need to breathe
I want to crave
What isn't mine
I want to bend
Twist in time

Foxgloves get flogged
Down a bitter street
It never makes sense
To create defeat
My hands glow with power
I feel corrupt
My mind fills with white noise
I self-destruct

Ignored

There's a light inside me
that sparkles and shines.
I turn towards the gold
of your bright eyes.
What will you do
when they see what you are?
What can you say
when you're bleeding for stars?
I wore the red dress;
I hoped you would see.
Now I sit in the dark, and
lick my wounds silently.

You decide

He glared around him and tried
not to fidget
Only time to kill
He never wasted his time on prayers
He no longer talked to god
He never liked the
answers he received
Here are where the vagabonds and
gypsies stray
The dressed up men and women, along
with those which are neither
or both
You hear someone scream
Then the same voice begs for
the pain to continue
I don't speak the language around here
I want to stand on the edge
but not jump in
your own fate
Bleeding is quicker than freezing

Empty Pockets

I can't wrap my head around it
so I sulk in the dark.
The mask is hard to keep in place
so you tear yours apart.
I twitch with anger but
on my hands I sat.
Never wear black if
you live with cats.
Maybe I will seem to start
to live clean, but you may
find things hidden between
the lines of my truth and yours.
"She's too friendly, probably a whore."
I can't believe or reject
your reality. What's true for
you may not be true for me.
It's a simple invitation to
your own private hell.
You accept it gladly.
You wear your relief well.
You tap me on the shoulder
searching for clue.
I empty my pockets, but
I have nothing for you.

Hideously Suggestive

There is a crooked house
in a room full of secrets.
I prayed like a machine
married to sickness.
If I made a mistake
I am a mistake.
Put me in a box and
I can't breathe.
Now comes a thrashing.
You were so good it
made me evil.
The stars are going out.
You gave me a sightless grin.
I drank tea with the hangman.
It was hideously suggestive—
the way he smiled at me.

Puffer Fish

The first fag of the day
always starts the morning
off right.
They eat metal then their
bodies make it safe.
He's just a puffer fish.
What if one day your dream
didn't need you.
You run away from the future.
Shiva, the Preserver entwined
with the destroyer.
Anger is the core of fear.
I'll never get done saving you.
There is no sword in your tongue.
There is no taint in your blood.
The rats are gnawing.
You were good, but you were
not right.

Smile the Insane

Since when did it
become so hard
to control
a shooting star
Since when did I
become so lost
When did all these
smells turn false
I didn't even
see it coming
I only saw how
fast she was running
And all of her words
mean nothing now
I really can't find
one person to blame
Knives in his right hand
smile the insane
smile of someone
with a full body shot
Sometimes he got lucky
and sometimes not
With his black trench coat
and his clothes all red
The preachers kneeling
have now wound up dead

Name

My beauty is only
Skin deep
Where will the
Children sleep
I owned my emotions
I owned my pain
I possessed it
I gave it a name

Warden

Chronic neck pain
comes from being hanged
in another life
You're always asking me
about that night
How it made me feel

There was a buzzing
It was all I could hear
Yelling in the background
I don't know how I knew
that the fire had taken control

Lumps of flesh
falling into the sea
skipping stones in the basement
It is the safest place to be

when the tornado hits
There's an insect clicking in my brain
Saw off my head and
fill it with razors
you're going to need to lie down

The warden guards us all

Monsoons

I listened for the voice of a god, but I didn't hear anything. There's not much left to do except chew me up and spit me out. But these monsoons are killing me. It seems I have spent all my life running from a mirage with your face. And the songs he sings tear me up inside. Do you feel sick? Cover your cough. I think of myself as a jackal—all smile with nothing underneath. My truth is filthier than a lie. I have no problem with the future; it's the past that haunts me. Talking to you is like talking to a machine.

Perfection

When the stars have dissolved
and the mountains depart
You will have time to
visit the crickets
The lilies she laid there
are now lost but
my heart is buried within these hills
There's a feather in my cap
My pupils are dilated
They leave you broken and singing
shuddering in a deep night
where nothing terrifies you more
than a full moon
My gaze injures you, I know

It's the little victories

The animalistic pride
of looking you in the eye
and challenging your sword
Can you take me at my word
Words are hollow things
Silence is fierce in its protest
I am parched and sleepy
You sell me your blood and
your breasts and the sky but
only on your terms
I am mad with the rhythm
of your labyrinth
You lurk under my skin
and burrow in my bones
I'll twist your perfection until
it is an ugly thing and
I can understand it

Ashen and Bloody

Something came out from the night
Ashen and bloody
Here the fight is the
dust of October
The star in the sky
is a lie
No judging these sharks—
Own your space
I feel the kettledrums
settle low in my body, and move
like the night ocean
I shiver with rage:
A cunt with teeth—
My crippled angel
You make a sound low in your throat
I am a fast leaner
But there was such pain in your eyes
Is it worse to have your moment—to
know your glory—
only to be denied?
Your words thrust deep inside
but I live for your smile
You always wanted to
bite down harder
Keep those impulses in check

Survival in the Scars

Gray was the color of her life.
Survival in the scars.
I am selling you, not your past.
If you have buried the most
awful secret, you will want to
remember where you put it.
One day I will drop out of the sky
and rip your world apart.
I found you in the words.
You summoned me and
then seduced me.
I find shelter in your anger.
Bleed away from me, and
I'll scream carefully.
Get a shovel.
Send out your best spies.
Listen with the part of your brain
that makes your hair stand on end.
Unlock memories.
We all move in circles.

Within

It corrupts from within,
this gold on my skin.
River beds are deep.
Monsters never sleep.
Neither do I, though
I cling to your sigh, and
remember every word
spoken that I never heard the
poison just beneath:
A tiger lily canopy.
Thunder and rain
until nothing remains.
I needed permission
almost a submission.
Spray me with sin.
Come diving in
the waters of lust
where seashells are dust,
and the corals are bone.

Hair

She stares at me
One hand over her eye
Pretending to take a picture
Pretending to try
Her lips pursed
With her casual grace
Wispy hair flying
Covering her face

Ireland

His colors flash
Across my mind
Dark pull scales
Twisting in time
My insides burn
With what I know
My body is broken
But I can't let go
Growing bigger
Every day
A gnawing feeling
That won't go away
Weight on my back
One fleeting glance
I could do better
Just one more chance
A timid suggestion
A timeless smile
Kiss all your pretty
Daydreams goodbye
It never will be
Quite like they say
But why does it always
End up this way
My hair got tangled
In your hands
Music from my heart
In Ireland
Making me tortured
Making me whole
Making me unlearn
These things I know

Eyelids of the Morning

It's not 100% true
Just true enough to be real
If you can't find a messiah
simply create your own
You are as beautiful as a
flower drinking the rain
Why focus on the facts
when the outcome is the same
Maybe it's a mistake
but it's mine to make
I'm in love with a shadow
You revisit the taste so you can
burn it in the fire when finished
You'll die for it
You'll kill for it
There's a poison inside
that numbs all the pain
Scars are so hard to read—
they tell of survival
The eyelids of the morning—
a hell of my own making

Maggots

The Morning Star
knows much about grace.
You're uneasy for an eternity.
Caught with your mask off
in the middle of a scene change.
You loved the devil's mind
and the animal within.
Soon the venom will hit your heart.
Something lives in your eyes.
You think that blood will heal the hunger,
but that's a well-kept secret
of finding yourself in the enemy's bed.
Even the sun seemed surprised.
In order to get to heaven,
you must get past the maggots
that tear the flesh apart.
They rape you with the sweetest
prayer on their lips.
It was then you learned fear.
You told the truth, and they
stripped you of your tongue.
It was then you learned to lie.

Easy

The blood flows easy
as my feet find the ground.
Your actions confuse me
but I don't make a sound.
As long as you're alive
you have a chance to be happy.
I can feel the wolf inside.
The fear only excites me.
Sometimes I see your face
inside my dream,
but it doesn't mean
a fucking thing

Crush Me

The air is thin here
It's harder to breathe
I was a victim of your
"Take no Casualties"

I said I needed you
It was no more than a lie
And now I cling here
Where old ghosts go to die

I screamed your name
But you never came
I screamed in pain
But you never came

I'll gather the minutes now
The days you took from me
And live for myself
And what I'll never be

You tried to name me
You tried to claim me
Then you maimed me
And always blamed me

No one will decide
What I will become
Strange and enchanted
With things I have not done

I was never her
No matter how hard you squeezed
And your voice in my head
Always seemed to crush me

GUILTY

I have built this thing.
I don't forget so
remember what I did for you.
Define guilty.
Anger is always self-centered.
Don't you get it?
There's nothing in the world that
cannot be negotiated.
I am healthy enough.
Fix yourself instead of someone else.
Never make the same mistake twice.
I don't know you like I want to, but
I'm not half the woman you are.
I fear what I cannot see.
You walk on feet that feel no pain.
Why should you be the one who pays
for doing the right thing?

I just made that last part up.

Civil War

There will be civil war
It's your satisfaction for
destruction
It's late at night and
The living are asleep but
the dead are awake

The dead and me

I'm stealing time
I gather it like fine sand
and shove it in my pockets
It smells like metallic honey
You enjoy your sickness
when it is self inflicted
You think death comes from
eating dead things
Your food has no flavor, but
every tool has a purpose
Your smile made muscles jerk
low in my stomach
Your eyes are like salt on a
wound
Take me to the edge of pain,
guilty until proven innocent

Surprise

I close my eyes tight
And open my arms wide
Grinning ear-to-ear
I accept your surprise
I wonder what
It could possibly be
Something magical and pretty
Something new to believe
But you left me waiting
Hands clutching the air
Waiting for a miracle
That just was not there
So my smile slowly fades
And I open my eyes
I never was any good
At hellos or goodbyes
You left an impression
That I just can't erase
Bitter disappointment
Is all I can taste

Your Face

Well, I thought about myself
Until the sickness poured in
But you spared me the rejection
Of telling me my faults then
I tried so much to block
Destiny in hand with fate
I wait until I'm half gone
Then wonder if I'm too late
But it really makes no difference
If you're mad you know you're mad
Staying up until light with you
I knew how much I had
Somehow you never fail
To slap me in my place
So why it is when I'm with him
I'm imagining your face?
He talked about himself
Until my ears bled
Every time I'm with him
I want you instead
I wait for some security
To come take me away
As you purify my entire being
To make the nightmares go away

Sink

It's so easy to forget.
I sink into the water
like a delirious Ophelia, and
know inside that seaweed makes
a poor pillow. Water makes you heavy.
They call me a dry drunk.
And you don't belong here.
I've been in this business since
the day I was born.
My beautiful enemy has
become a part of me.
Wolves shuttering—moving through the trees.
Monsters on the ocean floor
lumbered onward unnoticed.
We fought on a pirate's ship in a bathtub.
I let the lion out of its cage.
Shots rang out.
Guess what's on my paw?
It's obvious to me.
I'm evil, but I'm not to that level yet.
The brushing of your hand on
my arm was like an electric jolt, and
suddenly I didn't mind the rain.

Apollo

Apollo was wise to say nothing.
I can't say I was grateful.
I walked until my feet bled.
Out of spite, I was tarnished and hateful.
It may be a sin;
scars carved out of pain.
But I'd like to bring you back, so
I can kill you again.
I hope I am not contagious;
my vision is not clear.
I can't feel your hand,
but I know that you are near.
I grasp this pen,
hoping it will bleed for me.
Wish I could stop shaking.
Wish my heart would stop pounding.
I cannot read
because I cannot see.
Nothing will focus,
except blind insanity.

Ragnarok

I am here because my blood
is stained by the taint
of an enemy
I dared to be different from
those around me
When will it be your turn
to be cast out
They say I twist the truth
Disorder rages inside of me
Manipulating inner demons
As long as I am the problem
I am the solution
But if I'm saving the world
I need a decent shirt
It was a learned instinct
There's no real control
in loving
It's all about choices
I'm much better than
what I have been
They can't do this to me
Am I cursed for what
I could possibly do?
I do not fool myself that
I rule my destiny
It's easier to destroy
than to create
My heart turned blacker
than it already was
And my suffering was too
great for the world

Nasty Sense of Humor

She thinks she is so smart,
she is just horny and lonely.
The study of change can
make the rain stop
as I gasp for air.
I felt her emptiness—
a great echoing thing.
It blazed through my body and
made me want to fix it.
You know your worst nightmare
when you were young?
This is worse.
Evil is the part of us that wants
to hate without limit.
I could smell the liar in him.
I have a nasty sense of humor.
Just as the moon always changes her shape,
so do my emotions.
The hungry spider closes
on its victim.

Run

Come run with us sometime.
I know it's not your fault.
You always blame me, so you can
never take responsibility.
Not now.
Not like this.
I don't know what I was so
unhappy about.
What could I have been so
unhappy about?
You've always made poor decisions.
You feel so helpless.
You isolate yourself.
And you can be cold.
Life has made you hard.
I would give the world to you,
because it is your turn now.

Lucky Accident

I am an accident
Waiting to happen
Clutching your arm
Shaking and laughing
I knew the difference
Between a war and a storm
My eyes are flashing
You have been warned
Friends with the dawn
Running out of ink
Alone with a candle
Trying to think
Trying to decide
If it is worth it
If you are worthy
Or if I should quit
But your face won't leave
My aching mind
Like everyone else
She was one of a kind
You tell me I'm cold
But my flesh feels so hot
So everything is fine
But this voice screams "it's not"
So I bite my lip
Because I'm running out of ink
Running out of light
And running out of dreams

<u>Buried</u>

You will feel my scream
ripping through your veins.
So afraid to break.
Trying to stay awake.
And he took something
I did not want to give.
Crawling on my knees,
he made me beg.
In a nightmare
hopelessly trapped.
He took away something
I didn't know I had.
And I've spent half my life
trying to get it back.
When wolves get desperate
they sometimes attack.
He was feeding on fear, but
my sword cuts past the bone.
I will leave him dead here.
So, I cough up my life, and
he sinks like a stone.
A memory remains, but
the nightmare is gone.
And instead of a child,
there is a woman in the mirror.
My words rip out his heart, and
I'll bury him here.

Fight

These pictures crowding my mind do
not sale me on you,
or what you put me through.
One wrong move and the needle
sinks in.
I hold perfectly still, hoping not
to be stung.
You say your back hurts;
youth is wasted on the young.
I'm not in the best shape I've
been in my life.
But I'm not in the worst, and
I know how to fight.
Scream for me, scorpions;
you'll toss and turn.
The dead always remember
with fresh blood on their tongues.
In the end they all rot.
The trees look pitiful
as they tremble.
You're lucky the snakes
aren't that fast.

Fire In My Hand

Dull angels
Fight
Hire a demon
Greed aflame
Stalked down
Assault me with hunger
Naked in the mirror
With a stranger's grin
You brought horror and harm
The venom lurked beneath my pain
Tarnishes the mist
I can wait
With the patience of a mountain
My hands can only
Do so much
My guilt is a brick
Chained to my ankle
The Sandman is bold
But not asking for you
In my mind I see the burning
Swan as you whisper "they mate
For life"

Devil Behind You

I wanted someone to talk to.
Did you ever stop and think?
There's something moving through the dark.
Sometimes you can know too much history.
It walks in borrowed flesh.
Here you can find anything you can imagine.
Pray it doesn't find you first.
It wants to slash and stab
until nothing is left.
In this place even the trees bleed.
When you are constantly worrying the
devil is behind you
eventually you will see him
whether he is there or not.
But there's no such thing
as coming out of the rain.
A bullet rotates—
rips into organs.
If you save one, more will come.
Another, and another and everything you do
is never enough.

Grasp At Straws

Shit, he whispered with feeling:
You are a chore.
Just because you have the power
to play a god doesn't mean you should.
We appreciate time
because of our lack of it.
Nightmares warn you that something is wrong.
You watch me like a fox.
You behave like a shark in the water.
My howl is reduced to a whimper.
You are an odd ruin.
Depression is just anger turned inward.
Your tragic flaw
as you grasp at straws.
Why couldn't you just let me leave?
The purr of duct tape.
I speak to the trees.
Your tormented flowers glinted.
You'd tear the world apart
like a tiger in a paper cage.
Look in the mirror.
Somehow somewhere I am here
washing away bits of humanity.

Daisies For Judas

Your stare at yourself
memorizing the dew on your eyelashes.
You just can't seem to move,
no matter how much time passes.
And like love, people
can't seem to figure you out, but
the rage and the terror
were never what you were about.
I pick daisies for Judas,
willing him to live.
He begs others for mercy,
but it's himself he can't forgive.
How I pity the monster
with their dark hearts of stone,
waking up each sun-kissed morning
to discover they're alone.
We're all made of shards of light and dark.
Here in the shadows I can't tell us apart.
It was your silver-tipped tongue and
your flawless defense, but
now the blood's on my hands;
it simply makes no sense.
Your arrows circle blindly.
The scars you never mention.
The ink of dark allows you to
shoot straight with blind intention.
I am filled with labyrinths and
other strange wounds.
They choke me with their silence.
Sometimes they heal too soon.

www.ingramcontent.com/pod-product-compliance
Lightning Source LLC
Chambersburg PA
CBHW020500030426
42337CB00011B/173